AN IRISH ROADSIDE CAMERA

1907–1918

AN IRISH ROADSIDE CAMERA
1907–1918

The Years of Growth

Bob Montgomery

Dreoilín

For
Jean, Scott,
Robert and Andrew

BY THE SAME AUTHOR

An Irish Roadside Camera 1896-1906

Early Motoring in Ireland

Leslie Porter – Ireland's Pioneer Racing Driver

The Irish Grand Prix 1929-1931

The Phoenix Park Speed Trials 1903

The Irish Gordon Bennett Race 1903 (Dreoilín Album)

Ford Manufacture and Assembly at Cork 1919-1984

The 1903 Irish Gordon Bennett – The Race that Saved Motor Sport

Down Many a Road – The Story of Shell in Ireland 1902-2002

Published by Dreoilín Specialist Publications Limited,
Tankardstown, Garristown, County Meath, Ireland.

Trade enquiries to Dreoilín Specialist Publications Limited.
Telephone (+353 1) 8354481

First Published in October 2002

ISBN 1-902773-08-X
A CIP record for this title is available from the British Library

Design by Dreoilín Specialist Publications Limited,
set in Bembo by Computertype Limited
and printed in the Republic of Ireland by ColourBooks.

CONTENTS

INTODUCTION

The first volume of this series, *An Irish Roadside Camera – The Pioneering Years 1896-1906*, told the story of the early years of motoring in Ireland for the first time. It did so by the use of evocative photographs drawn from many differing sources. I chose to tell our motoring history in this visual fashion because it has always seemed to me that Irish people have a particular fascination for old photographs. Perhaps, because so much of the detail of our history has been lost, old photographs evoke a strong reaction amongst us, and properly contextulised, they can bring a tale such as this to life in a way words alone cannot do.

And so it proved with the first volume of *An Irish Roadside Camera*. Suffice to say that the reaction to the first volume was such as to ensure that there would be successive volumes. This ncw offering covering the years between 1907 and 1918, which I have called *The Years of Growth*, is the first result. On this occasion the majority of the photographs are drawn from the Archive of the Royal Irish Automobile Club with many coming from the pages of *The Motor News* magazine, as do the wonderfully evocative drawings from the pen of Oswald

Motor millinery

Cunningham. These photographs and drawings have not been seen by the public for between eighty-five and ninety-four years, the length of time since they were first published. They tell a story which is part of our social history and which has, for too long, been part of a hidden history.

Throughout this book I have used the title 'The Great War' to describe what is more usually called today the 'First World War' and which took place between 1914 and 1918. I have used this in preference to the latter title as I feel that, although the horrors of this war have long since been surpassed, it resonates with the way this terrible conflict affected all those who lived through it. It is a name of the time, and as such its use here is as valid as the motoring terms of the time that I have used throughout this book.

I hope that you, the reader, will once again enjoy this small effort to reclaim a part of our history which has been ignored for too long.

Bob Montgomery,
September 2002.

LIST OF PHOTOGRAPHS

CHRONOLOGY OF MOTORING IN IRELAND
1907–1918

1907   Irish Automobile Club (IAC) Motor Show held at the RDS
Second IAC Reliability Trial
Road signposts provided by IAC
First Ford Model N cars go on sale in Ireland. By 1913, some 600 Ford's representing 10% of total car sales are sold in the Irish market

1908   Second and final Irish Automobile Club Show at the RDS
Third IAC Reliability Trial

1909   Society of Motor Manufacturers and Traders (SMMT) forbid their members from becoming involved in the proposed 1909 IAC Motor show, thus effectively killing it off. (In fact, it is not until 1976 that Motor Shows at the RDS are revived).
Fourth IAC Reliability Trial

1910   Cars first taxed on hp ratings
Proposal for 6 mph speed limit in Dublin fails

1911   Irish branch of the SMMT established

1913   Rosslare Speed Trials. A speed of 107 mph set up S T Robinson
Motorist's associations pressure Local Government Roads Board for road improvements
'Best' petrol retails for 1s 9d a gallon (about 11 cents). This included 3d duty.

1914   IAC Irish Light Car Trials
Ambulence service set-up by IAC members. In service until 1918
Kenelm Lee Guinness drives a Sunbeam to victory in the Tourist Trophy Race on the Isle of Man

1915   Petrol in limited supply

1916   IAC ambulances in operation during the Easter Rising
Ford purchases 136 acre site at Cork to establish factory

1917   Henry Ford & Son incorporated with registered offices at 36 South Mall, Cork
Work begins on construction of Ford's Marina plant

1918   IAC receives Royal patronage for humatarian services during the War

THE GUINNESS SEGRAVE LIBRARY
AND ARCHIVE OF
THE ROYAL IRISH AUTOMOBILE CLUB

The RIAC Guinness Segrave Library and Archive was established in 1985 with the generous support of the 3rd Earl of Iveagh. The Library commemorates two members of the Guinness family, Sir Algernon and his brother Kenelm, who together with their contemporary, Sir Henry Segrave, were amongst the first Irish drivers to carve out an international reputation for themselves in the exacting world of motor sport.

The Library contains many rare volumes including 'runs' of Mecredy's *The Irish Cyclist* and *The Motor News*. That other early Irish journal, *The Irish Wheelman*, is also well represented within the Library, which also includes 'runs' of the more usual journals of record, *The Autocar, The Motor, Motor Sport, Speed* and of more recent times, *Autosport*. As such, the RIAC Guinness Segrave Library is an important collection of motoring literature, while its material relating to early Irish motoring is quite unique, and because Ireland took centre stage in the world of motorsport at the time of the 1903 Gordon Bennett Race, the Irish International Grand Prix series from 1929-31 and during the golden age of the Tourist Trophy series from 1928 to 1936, its value as an important motoring archive is greatly enhanced.

Since 1985 the Library has continued to grow through further gifts of motoring literature and its collection of photographs, programmes and other motoring memorabilia has reached the stage that this now forms an important archive in itself. The library is not open to the public but access is given to bone-fide researchers through the RIAC's Archive Curator. It is also hoped to develop further the Dreoilín series of Transport Albums in association with the Archive, to extend over a wide range of transport related subjects of Irish interest.

If you would like to assist the Archive's work of preserving Ireland's unique motoring heritage, why not join the 'Friends of the Archive Group' - details from The Curator, RIAC Archive, 34 Dawson Street, Dublin 2.

GROWING PAINS

If the period from 1896 to 1906 can be accurately described as the pioneering years of Irish motoring, then the succeeding period from 1907 to 1918 may undoubtedly be given the title '*the years of growth*'. During this short span of years the automobile in Ireland went from being a sporting curiosity owned by a privileged few to a veritable maid-of-all-work, becoming relatively commonplace throughout even the remoter parts of this island. The impetus to its development created by The Great War (1914-1918) secured its place in our society and provided many thousands with their first opportunity to drive a motor vehicle while serving in the British armed services. This in turn provided a ready supply of drivers and mechanics as well as giving the urge to great numbers to aspire to ownership of a car after the conflict. The war also led to the rapid development of the motor vehicle for farm use. Hithertofore, cars had been adapted for use to draw ploughs and other work upon the farm. The few specially constructed farm vehicles were large and cumbersome and it was not until the development of Henry Ford's tractor design in the second half of the Great War that rapid progress was made in this field. Indeed, Ford undertook the construction of the first dedicated plant to produce tractors in the world at Cork, although it was mid-1919 before this plant was completed, too late for its products to make a difference to wartime food production.

The adaptability of the motor vehicle, now more commonly simply called the 'car', led to its adoption for

'*Are you hurt, Michael? Shall I go for a doctor?*'
'*It's not a doctor I want; bring me a lawyer!*'

a wide variety of uses. By the end of 1918, the car and its commercial derivatives, was being used as a taxi, for postal deliveries, military and hospital use as well as for fire engines. Cars and buses had become commonplace and sporting trials were a highly regarded way of testing the comparative strengths, and indeed, weaknesses, of manufacturer's latest products. Touring became a popular and acceptable pastime. Indeed, the car revolutionised tourism, a development long foreseen by the father of Irish motoring, R J Mecredy, who had been a lone prophet of Irish tourism from the 1880s when he first championed the ability of the cycle to open up this land to tourist development.

The success of the Dublin Motor Shows organised by the pioneering Irish Automobile Club in 1907 and 1908 was a good indicator of how the car had been assimilated into Irish society and while car ownership was still confined to the more well-off in our society, the vast influx of personnel from the armed forces after the war who were able to drive – a freedom they didn't want to lose – ensued that before long this desire would be fulfilled by more affordable products from the car manufacturers.

All of this progress came at a price. Fatalities in road accidents increased and were a cause of great upset to many of the pioneers. Horse-drawn traffic mixed with car traffic in the cities, often with lamentable results and the early freedom which motoring had represented gave way to ever increasing legislation designed to control the movement of cars. The car, for better or worse, was clearly on the road to becoming the most consequential product of the twentieth century

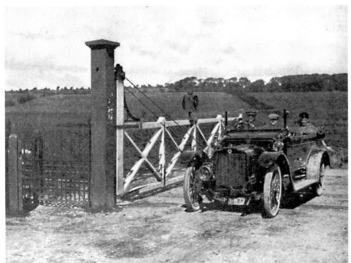

(1) Killarney and back in a day on a Brasier – 1911

In 1911, the English manager of the *Societie des Automobiles Brasier*, M André Jouve, and his Dublin agent, John Colclough, suggested to the editor of the *Motor News* that it was perfectly feasible to travel in one of their cars from Dublin to Killarney and back in a day's driving. To much interest by the Press, the journey was successfully completed, despite taking the wrong road near Newcastle, County Limerick. The Brasier, which performed faultlessly, is photographed crossing the Killarney to Limerick railway line at Rathmore, County Kerry. The journey of 367 miles was completed in eighteen hours.
Source: RIAC Archive

(2) Dr Tweedy of the Rotunda Hospital on his 8 hp Rover – 1908

A motoring medical man. Dr Tweedy of the Rotunda Hospital, Dublin, photographed on his 8 hp Rover car.
Source: RIAC Archive

(3) Dublin's Champion Motor Trappist – 1911

'*Dublin's champion motor trappist*' was the title bestowed upon Sergeant Kenoy of the Dublin Metropolitan Police whose pursuit of erring Dublin motorists was of legendary status. The good sergeant is pictured in conversation at the Bohemian Football Club ground.
Source: RIAC Archive

(4) Miss Hazel West and her 10/12 hp Peugeot – 1908

Miss Hazel West of Kilcroney, Bray, was a well-known Irish sportswoman when she purchased a 10/12 hp Peugeot in 1908. After a few short lessons, she drove the Peugeot from Bridgewater to Holyhead, *en route* to Ireland, during which she fell into a police speed trap, an incident which was to cost her three pounds. Back home in Ireland she employed a mechanic for three weeks to give her instruction in the mechanical intricacies of the Peugeot, thereafter carrying out all maintenance herself.
Source: RIAC Archive

21

(5) The IAC Motor Show at Ballsbridge – 1908
A general view of the Irish Automobile Club's Motor Show held at the premises of the Royal Dublin Society at Ballsbridge in January 1908. The Show was very successful and amongst the many makes that can be seen in this photograph are Argyll, Humber, Rover, Berliet, Cadillac and Sunbeam.
Source: RIAC Archive

(6) An up-to-date Bread Van – 1908
During the early part of the last century, and certainly up to the Great War, it was common practice to convert older cars into commercial or farm vehicles and many examples which would be greatly prized today, ended their days in this fashion. This early Daimler was converted in 1908 into a bread van for the firm of John Beattie, Bakers and Confectioners, of Dundalk. It must surely be unique as probably the first and only time a Daimler became a bread van.
Source: RIAC Archive

(7) F Eastmead during the Sunbeam End-to-end Trial – 1907

The first decade of the last century was the hey-day of 'trials' of all sorts designed to prove the reliability and strength of various makes of car. A common trial was driving non-stop from one end of Ireland to the other, and sometimes back again as well. This Sunbeam is engaged on such a trial in 1907 and is seen midway through one half of its successful journey outside the telegraph office at Dublin's General Post Office. Its driver was F Eastmead and it successfully completed the Trial.

Source: RIAC Archive

(8) A dash through the Flood at Clontarf – 1909

The seafront at Clontarf is prone to flooding, as residents there can attest even today. That this was so long ago as April 1909 is demonstrated by this photograph of James O'Connor KC, driving his car through a flood. Following thirty-two hours of continuous rain the road flooded and the tramway service had to be suspended, while breaches had to be made in the seawall to allow the water to escape. Only a small number of cars proved able to traverse the flood conditions.

Source: RIAC Archive

(9) A pair of Soap-box Cars – 1909

Almost for as long as cars have been produced, 'soap-box' cars have been built by boys aspiring to future car ownership. These two youths from Tobercurry, County Sligo, had the skill and enthusiasm to build two worthy examples. They were reported to be '*not good hill climbers, but terrors to go downhill*'. Interestingly the boys have selected a London index mark for their cars. Was there a particular locally based London-registered car they admired or does this reflect the high percentage of London registered cars then extant in Ireland?
Source: RIAC Archive

(10) Motorcars at the Dublin Horse Show – 1909

A sure sign of the acceptance of the motor car into Irish Society was the growth of the car park at the Ballsbridge Show Grounds of the Royal Dublin Society. This selection of fine motor cars was photographed at the 1909 Dublin Horse Show and includes several Daimlers, very much the preferred choice of polite Irish society.
Source: RIAC Archive

(11) Taking the Hounds to the Hunt – 1914
A photograph taken at a Meet of the Muskerry Hunt, County Cork, showing the specially-bodied vehicle used for transporting the hounds when the meet was any distance from the kennels.
Source: RIAC Archive

(12) Motors for Hire – 1907

The range of cars available for hire from Messrs. Thompson's Motor Car Company outside their premises at Great Brunswick Street, Dublin. The cars are (from left): 20/24 hp Clement Talbot, side-entrance, cape cart hood; 16/22 hp Gladiator, side-entrance, cape cart hood; 12/16 hp Clement Talbot, landaulette; 12/16 hp Clement Talbot, side entrance, cape cart hood; 12/16 hp Clement Talbot, side entrance, cape cart hood; 3-cylinder 10/12 hp Panhard, side entrance and hood.
Source: RIAC Archive

EVERYDAY USE

As the number of cars on the road began to dramatically increase from 1905/6 onwards, they, not surprisingly, began to find a multitude of new uses. Commercial use of the car developed quickly and while prior to 1906 such use was mainly confined to taxi services, a small number of motor bus services and a sprinkling of cars converted into delivery vehicles, after that date new uses seemed to appear almost daily. At the same time the development of chars-a-banc opened up the possibility of trips to beauty spots such as Glendalough in County Wicklow for many who previously could only visit locations served by train. The char-a-banc excursion became a popular outing, even if, on occasion at least, it could be wet and draughty owing to the open and unprotected nature of the vehicle. And while Belfast waited until 1909 for its first Taxi cab, cars were being used for weddings by 1908, and for funerals within a year or two of that. Also, by 1909, a number of local authorities had also purchased Fire Engines, although few were as advanced as the 50 hp Leyland of Dublin Corporation pictured on page 31.

Doctors were amongst the first to embrace the use of the car in the course of their profession, and the motor industry seems to have directed a lot of its effort towards convincing medical doctors of the practicality of employing a car for their 'rounds'. The car soon found widespread acceptance amongst the medical profession, no doubt helped, as my colleague John S Moore has pointed out, by the fact that they received a discount from chemists from where supplies of motor spirit were bought in the early days.

The other significant factor in bringing about the large increase in car numbers in Ireland was their ever improving reliability. By 1911, it had been demonstrated that it was possible to comfortably travel between Dublin and Killarney in a day, while wintry conditions, although always ready to catch out the unwary, could be confidently tackled by a thoughtful driver.

One particularly interesting aspect in relation to Irish motorists was the relatively high proportion of lady drivers amongst their number as well as the large contingent who carried out their own maintenance covering items such as lubricating, cleaning and general servicing. Contemporary magazine reports affirm this unexpected attribute of Irish motorists.

(13) The Shamrock Motor Bus – 1907
The 'Shamrock' motor bus was shown at the Dublin Motor Show in January 1907 and remained in Dublin for a period afterwards carrying out demonstration runs. In this photograph it is being used to transport the Irish Rugby Team to an international match at Lansdowne Road from the Hotel Metropole from which it is shown starting out.
Source: RIAC Archive

(14) A Wedding photo – 1909
Perhaps one of the first uses of a car at a wedding? A J Power and his bride are the happy couple aboard the former's Berliet car. Incidentally, it was also around this time that the first recorded use of the car as a hearse in Ireland occurs.
Source: RIAC Archive

(15) A Motor Funeral – 1914
While by 1914, the motor hearse was quite common, a motor funeral was still rare in 1914 when this procession was photographed in Belfast.
Source: RIAC Archive

(16) A Motor Ambulance for Hire – 1912
The enterprising firm of Messrs Thompson's Motor car Company added to their fleet of hire vehicles, an ambulance fitted out on a 28 hp Daimler chassis. The *Motor News* reported: '*Dublin's high reputation in surgical matters brings to the city a number of persons who are compelled to undergo operations, and to those who under such circumstances have to be conveyed from the train, or direct from their own residences, to the operating room, this new vehicle, to use a hackneyed phrase, fills a long-felt want.*' *Source: RIAC Archive*

(17) C M O'Brien MD – 1909

One of the first to use a car in the Dublin area for his work
was Dr C M O'Brien of 29 Merrion Square. The good doctor,
here photographed with his two sons, Barry and Esmonde, on
his 15/20 hp Unic, also found time to be '*an all-round good shot,
a keen golfer, and an experienced mountain climber and traveller*'. His
smartly turned-out chauffeur is interestingly part of the
photograph, even if placed in the background. Photographs of
the period seldom show the chauffeur in anything other than a
stiffly posed position in the drivers seat, usually staring straight
ahead, as if a part of the car.

Source: RIAC Archive

(18) Belfast's first Taxi Cab – 1909

Taxi cabs, in Dublin since at least 1907, didn't come to Belfast
until October 1909, this photograph portraying the city's first
such vehicle.

Source: RIAC Archive

(19) 50 hp Leyland Fire Engine of Dublin Corporation – 1909
This magnificent vehicle was the new 50 hp Leyland Fire Engine of Dublin Corporation's Dublin Fire Department. The Lancashire manufacturer was one of the first to see the commercial potential of specialist vehicles such as this.
Source: RIAC Archive

(20) Ambulance of Dublin Fire Brigade – 1914
This fine 20 hp Leyland Ambulance entered service with Dublin Fire Brigade in January 1914. The body could carry four injured persons, two attendents and the driver.
Source: RIAC Archive

(21) Dublin Traffic – 1911
A scene of utter traffic chaos in Dublin's Dame street on the day of the King's Garden Party at the Viceregal Lodge. The Dublin Metropolitan Police were the recipients of bitter criticism for scenes such as this.
Source: RIAC Archive

(22) 25 hp Karrier Char-a-banc – 1911
The firm of Marshall of Dublin provided a range of commercial vehicles for hire, including this 25 hp Karrier char-a-banc here being used to convey the staff of a caterers to Portmarnock for an outing to a golf tournament. In the background can be seen one of Marshall's Mail vans which were contracted to carry the mails between sorting offices.
Source: RIAC Archive

(23) *En-route* to Punchestown – 1912
An interesting photograph of a Darracq car passing a Commer char-a-banc at the Johnstown Inn on the Naas Road while *en-route* to the horse races at Punchestown. The varied nature of the road surface can be clearly seen.
Source: RIAC Archive

(24) J H Robinson's 20 hp Ford towing an Aeroplane – 1912
During the Autumn of 1912, the aviator James Valentine, made a number of demonstration flights around the country in his Deperdussin monoplane, being towed between locations by the 20 hp Ford of J H Robinson. Novel as this method of transporting the aeroplane may have seemed at the time, C S Rolls had used a car to tow his balloon and its equipment some years earlier.
Source: RIAC Archive

(25) Wintry conditions at Calary Bog – 1909
A photograph taken opposite Calary Schoolhouse following heavy snow and showing the Sugar Loaf in the background. Cars of this period probably had reasonably good traction in such conditions owing to their narrow tyres and low power outputs.
Source: RIAC Archive

(26) Watching the Polo from the car – 1912
Some twenty thousand people witnessed the final of the Irish County Polo Championship in the Phoenix Park, Dublin. Some, at least, as is apparent in this photograph of two Daimlers, watched the game from their cars.
Source: RIAC Archive

(27) An adventurous motorist on Lough Derg – 1917
A particularly severe winter in 1916/17 led to Lough Derg being frozen for the first time in twenty-two years (yes, winters were harder then!). This adventurous (perhaps foolhardy?) motorist has ventured onto the ice in his 10 hp Calcott. History does not record the outcome.
Source: RIAC Archive

(28) In Dawson Street, Dublin – 1909
The showrooms of Messrs. J Hutton & Sons in Dawson Street, Dublin. The white Daimler in the foreground belonged to Richard Croker of Glencairn, Dublin, otherwise infamous as 'Boss Croker'. Dawson Street was one of the main locations of motor showrooms in Dublin.
Source: RIAC Archive

(29) The Royal Commission on Congestion – 1907
During the work of the Royal Commission on Congestion in Ireland, the members of the Commission travelled over 20,000 miles using four Brown cars. The Brown cars apparently performed faultlessly apart from the expected punctures and it was noted that the only town in Ireland where they had failed to obtain petrol was Belmullet, attesting to the already widespread distribution of petrol as early as 1907. Three of the cars were photographed in Boyle, and while the names of the drivers were not recorded, those occupying the back seats were (from left): Sir John Columb MP; the Earl of Dudley; McM Cavanagh; Angus Sutherland; Conor O'Kelly MP and Walter Callan.
Source: RIAC Archive

(30) Tyres and Golf Balls – 1914
A 15 hp Napier delivery van specially built for the Dunlop Company in Dublin. Note the promotion of Dunlop golf balls complete with giant ball on its roof.
Source: RIAC Archive

'IRISH MADE'

As a predominantly rural island, Ireland didn't contribute largely to the lists of motor manufacturers extant across Europe in the early years of the last century. Those that did venture into the design and manufacture of motor vehicles found the going uniformly tough and with the notable exception of Chambers, all disappeared from manufacturing at an early stage. Being Ireland, there were, of course, some glorious failures, but it was not until the establishment of Henry Ford & Son at Cork in mid-1919 (ironically, initially as a tractor factory) that manufacture on anything approaching a large scale came into being here. That enterprise and its unique story, however, falls outside the parameters of this work and must wait for a future volume.

Of those that did attempt manufacture, the Chambers brothers stand supreme. Having been involved in the design of the Vauxhall car, Jack Chambers designed and built the first Chambers car in 1904. Unconventional in its layout, it introduced several new ideas to car production. Success in the Irish and Scottish Reliability Trials over the next few years led to Chambers designs achieving a good reputation and the business prospered as new models were added to their range. At its height, production of Chambers cars was probably no more than five hundred cars per year and although the cars gained a good reputation for craftsmanship, this was not sufficient to save the company in the harsh economic climate that prevailed following the Great War. Production of Chambers cars finally ceased in 1924.

Another of the 'one-off' cars produced as a prelude to production, and which failed to go any further, was the Alesbury produced in 1907 by the Alesbury Brothers of Edenderry and exhibited at the Irish Automobile Club Motor Show in January of that year. This car never made it into production and the Alesbury Brothers instead built up a strong business manufacturing car wheels for various British car makers. The Fergus was a product of J B Ferguson (brother of Harry) and was aimed at the American market. Displayed there in 1916, the Fergus generated much interest but plans for worthwhile production came to naught.

The Burke Engineering and Motor Company of Clonmel were another firm that aspired to car manufacture. In 1906 they produced prototypes of 10/12 hp and 24/30 hp cars. No more than five cars were produced and the company went into liquidation in 1910.

The remaining design of note is perhaps the most remarkable. Philip Townsend Sommerville-Large had been a railway engineer before his retirement to Kilcullen, County Kildare. In 1907 he began construction of a car to be built to his own design. Although the car used a large number of readily available parts, many of them were extensively modified to his own specifications. Using a Gnome six-cylinder engine and a MAB chassis with a body he designed himself, the car was finally completed in 1909. The result was a magnificent vehicle which would have proven a worthy competitor to Rolls-Royce. Only this prototype was built and happily it survives today at the Museum of Irish Transport at Killarney. The high cost of its production is usually given as the reason for the Silver Stream not going into manufacture, but a close examination of the original costs does not seem to support this contention.

(31) Messrs. Chambers Motors Erecting Shop – 1918
The Erecting Shop, or Assembly room of Chambers Motors at their Cuba Street factory in Belfast shows both cars and bottle wiring machines – the company's other successful product – being assembled.
Source: RIAC Archive

(32) A 12/16 hp Chambers delivered to F A Kenny – 1915
Purchased new by Mr F A Kenny of Fynagh, County Galway, this 12/16 hp Chambers was the latest model to appear from the Belfast manufacturer in 1915. Fitted with a '*five-seater body of the streamline type*', it came complete with spare wheel, and was fitted with CAV Lighting with generator and batteries. It's appearance was described as '*leaving nothing to be desired, it being finished in a buff colour, with the mudguards in black*'.
Source: RIAC Archive

(33) In Furze Glen, Phoenix Park – 1912
Jack Chambers photographed in the company's 1912 5-seater tourer in the Furze Glen in Dublin's Phoenix Park.
Source: RIAC Archive

(34) Mr Kenneth on a Burke car – *c.*1907
The Burke Engineering and Motor Company of Clonmel were another firm that aspired to car manufacture. Between 1906 and 1909 they produced several prototypes of 10/12 hp and 24/30 hp cars, but it is almost certain that no more than five cars were produced and the company went into liquidation in 1910.
Source: RIAC Archive

(36) BGR Hydraulic Jack – 1917
Irish ingenuity was evident in the BGR Hydraulic Jack
marketed by Messrs Victor Robb Limited of Chichester Street,
Belfast, and designed by their works manager, G Bowman. The
'BGR' Jack is here shown fitted to a 12/16 hp Sunbeam car
and clearly shows the car raised on four shafts, which were
operated by a mechanically-actuated double-acting force pump
fitted to the top of the gearbox housing.
Source: RIAC Archive

(35) The 'Gimbal' Farm Tractor – 1917
Before the layout of the tractor as we know it
was established by Henry Ford in 1915, many
different approaches were taken by inventors
to making a mechanical tractor. S J Murphy
of Drogheda produced the 'Gimbal' Farm
Tractor, an interesting design which
incorporated four-wheel drive. It was claimed
to be capable of ploughing two nine-inch
furrows at an average rate of $3^1/_2$ miles an
hour.
Source: RIAC Archive

(37) The Silver Stream – 1908
Philip Somerville Large's magnificent
prototype, the Silver Stream, happily surrvives
today on display at the Museum of Irish
Transport, Killarney, County Kerry.
Source: Museum of Irish Transport

Surprisingly, given the slower start to motoring in Ireland than in Britain, the commercial appendages of motoring – car showrooms, bus and taxi services, car repair works, the trade use of motor vehicles, motor ambulances and large load carrying vehicles – established themselves comparatively quickly here.

The first motor bus service in Ireland was almost certainly the Enniscrone to Ballina service operated with ten-seater Daimler cars and established by a syndicate in 1901, while W F 'Bill' Peare established the first purpose-built garage in Ireland at Catherine Street, Waterford, in 1901. (The first motor company to be established in Ireland was almost certainly The Northern Motor company at Chichester Street, Belfast, which was founded by Leslie Porter and George Coombe in 1899).

Contrary to popular myth, the majority of garages established were just that, garage businesses established to service the motor trade and not as is popularly believed, blacksmiths who turned their hand from horses to the new-fangled automobile. Most of those who began garage businesses could claim at least some background of training and experience in the repair of motor vehicles, often in Britain or abroad. Car showrooms sprang up in the more fashionable streets of Dublin and Belfast as well as in Cork, Limerick, Waterford and Galway. In Dublin these showrooms were centred on Grafton and Dawson Streets while Great Brunswick Street, now Pearse Street, became the centre of automotive suppliers such as the many tyre and battery companies then extant. (Indeed, the facias of several of the purpose-built shop-fronts on Pearse Street still exist and are clearly visible on what is today a dreary and run-down thoroughfare.

Commercial vehicles, delivery vans and lorries, were slower to become established in the Irish streetscape. Most delivery vans were, in the early years, coach-built conversions from private cars which were past their best years. By 1905/6, however, the value of small and medium sized delivery vans was well established and most car manufacturers offered at least one such model in their range. Purpose-built larger load carrying vehicles were a much less common sight on Irish roads and this undoubtedly reflected the lack of a manufacturing infrastructure in what was then a predominantly rural economy. Without the widespread need for this sort of load-carrying capacity, a high proportion of the vehicles which did find their way onto Irish roads were employed either directly in agriculture or in trade associated with it. Some of the more progressive landowners embraced the new motor technology and it is particularly interesting to view the many motor machines designed to facilitate farm work which were the product of Irish inventors. A large number of these were motorised tractors that preceded the laying down of the 'modern' tractor layout with which we are familiar by Henry Ford in the second decade of the last century.

(38) Kilkenny-Callan Motor Service – 1912
The early 1910s saw the inauguration of many public omnibus services. Usually, they were the result of a far-seeing business syndicate spotting a business opportunity but sometimes, as in the case of the Kilkenny to Callan service, they were due to the enterprise of the local people. This service was operated successfully by Messrs Lambert and Company, motor engineers in Kilkenny and employed this 20/30 hp Milnes-Daimler motor bus which was fitted with a train carriage style eighteen seater body built by the Edenderry firm of Messrs Alesbury Brothers.
Source: RIAC Archive

(39) The new Char-a-banc of the Southern Coaching Company – 1916
Following the liquidation of the Tourist Development Syndicate Limited, which prior to the beginning of the Great War had operated a successful coaching service linking the termini of the Great Southern and Western Railways in Cork and Kerry with the major hotels of the area, a new company, The Southern Coaching Company was formed in 1916 to operate this service. It's first vehicle, a 40 hp Caledon chassis with a twenty-five seat char-a-banc body (supplied by Messrs Thompson's Motor Car Company Limited of Dublin) is here pictured on a trial run in the Wicklow mountains with members of the hotel and tourist industry being treated to a demonstration of its abilities.
Source: RIAC Archive

(40) One of Dublin's new Motor Buses – 1908

In 1908 Dublin streets reverberated to the sound of new motor buses. In this photograph, taken on St. Stephen's Green at the top of Grafton Street, the bus, which carries an English registration, is most probably a Wolseley 'H' model which had a 30 hp engine with final drive by means of roller chains.

Source: RIAC Archive

(41) Irish Motor Traders in Conference – 1916

Members of the Belfast and District Branch of the Motor Trade Association photographed at their conference at Londonderry in 1916.
Top row: G E Fulstow (Anglo-American Oil Co.); H Roberts (City of Derry Garage); W McCammond (North of Ireland Motor Co., Belfast); T Johnston (Anglo-American Oil Co.); J Gallagher (Manager, C E Jacob, Belfast); H Simpson (Simpson and Co., Portrush); C Taylor (Vacuum Oil Co., Belfast); Dan Lynn, Cushendall.
Second row: R Stewart (Stewart Bros., Portrush); J Steen (Martin and Steen, Limavady); C Mitchell (Ramelton); H Whitehead (Whitehead and Co., Belfast); D Levinson (National Motor Co., Clones); H Barker (Vacuum Oil Co., Belfast); J White (White Bros., Omagh); J G McMullan (Preston and Co.).
Third row: W A Ludlow (Shell Co.); J Stuart, Coleraine; J Stuart jnr.,

Coleraine; J Sheppard (Ulster Motor Works; R Hamilton (Manager, Alexander Motor Co., Londonderry); J Spence, Belfast; S Taggart, Londonderry; Wm. McMullan (Preston and Co.); W Denby, Belfast; J Maguire, Enniskillen; R Chambers, Belfast; J Smyth (Mervue Motor Garage).
Fourth row: J Boyd (local sec., MTA); J A Taylor (Manager, Dunlop Rubber Co., Dublin); W Quigley, Londonderry; R G Wilkenson (Thompson's Motor Car Co.); J W Buchanan, Strabane; H Ferguson, Belfast (President); M McDermott, Dungiven; A Stringer, Belfast; R A Martin, Limavady; F A Mawhinney (J B Ferguson Ltd.); F J Gill (Monogram Oil Co.).
Front row (sitting): D D Pyper (Wood-Milne Tyre Co.); G Birch (Birch and Workman Ltd.); R Workman (Birch and Workman Ltd.).
Source: RIAC Archive

(42) Electric Delivery Van for the Dublin Bread Company – 1908
Electric delivery vans became popular during this period for short city deliveries. The Dublin Bread Company was one of the first to see the potential of this type of vehicle for their business. This Lotis delivery van was built for them by Messrs Sturmey Motors Limited of Coventry and supplied by the Ampere Electrical and Motor Engineering Company of Fleet Street, Dublin. Electric bread delivery vans remained in operation in Dublin right up to the 1980s when the last were withdrawn from service.
Source: RIAC Archive

(43) Two of the Peugeot delivery vans in use by Messrs. Eason & Sons – 1911
The fast delivery of newspapers has always been a prerequisite of the business of Messrs Eason & Sons of Dublin, a company happily still flourishing today. In 1911, they operated a fleet of fast Peugeot delivery vans, two of which were photographed outside one of their branch shops.
Source: RIAC Archive

(44) Two Halley vans used on the Dublin-Kells Motor Mail Service – 1912
By the end of the first decade of the last century, the Royal Mail had begun to contract out for motorised mail services between various key locations in Ireland. The two 20 hp Halley vans pictured here were operated by Mr W Donne Marshall of Rutland Square, Dublin, and did a daily run between Dublin and Kells, a distance of about 80 miles. One vehicle was held in reserve as a back-up but the Halley proved most reliable in use.
Source: RIAC Archive

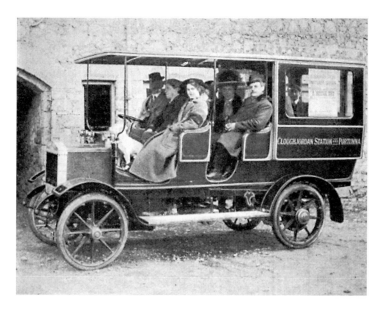

(45) Cloughjordan Motor Bus – 1912
The Cloughjordan Motor Bus Service began operating this Straker-Squire vehicle between Cloughjordan Railway Station and Portumna in February 1912. The bus picked up and set down passengers anywhere along its route which it travelled twice daily in each direction. It had room for five passengers and their luggage. It was unusual in having a large closed-in section at the rear for luggage and parcels.
Source: RIAC Archive

(46) Derry's new motor Char-a-banc – 1912
A 30 hp Lacre char-a-banc began operating a bus and mail service between Londonderry and Greencastle in June 1912. The mail service was the first of its kind in Northern Ireland and it was reported that great crowds turned out along the route to see its initial run, during which the Lecre carried a full compliment of twenty-four passengers. *Source: RIAC Archive*

(47) The Grafton Motor Company premises – 1912
In the period with which this book is concerned, the motor trade in Ireland made its home in Dublin's fashionable Grafton and Dawson Streets, while the automotive accessory businesses were grouped primarily in Great Brunswick Street, now Pearse Street. One of the best known of the motor showrooms was that of the Grafton Motor Company in Grafton Street. About a dozen cars were usually on display in the well-lighted showrooms, and one was likely to see examples of such well-known makes as Wolseley, Metallurgique, Minerva, Darracq, Humber and Flanders, for all of which makes the Grafton Motor Company was an agent. The company also catered for motor cyclists and had a large selection of motoring clothing available for prospective purchasers.
Source: RIAC Archive

(48) A view of the interior of Messrs Waytes Garage at Portobello – 1915
Messrs Ben and Albert Waytes first set up as motor engineers in Lemon Street, Dublin, in the first few years of the 1900s. Their business prospered and grew and the premises were added to several times until by 1914 it became necessary to purchase a new site for their operations. A plot of land was purchased beside the canal at Portobello Bridge and a new purpose-built garage was constructed there. (Incidentally, the Lemon Street premises was retained to cater for their cycle business). Waytes operated a Taxi service from these premises as well as a repair shop. In later years this building became the home of Messrs Brittains, the Morris agents in Ireland and the assembly of a wide variety of Morris vehicles was carried out there. *Source: RIAC Archive*

NO HAZARDS for TAXIS in DUBLIN.

——— 'PHONE 1597. ———

No Hazards or risks with

A & B TAXIS

10d. PER MILE, 2 6 MINIMUM CHARGE.

New Taxis, Speaking Tubes, Electric Light.

——————

4/- per hour while Standing.   Careful Drivers in Uniform.

WAYTE BROS.,
11 & 12 LEMON STREET, GRAFTON ST.

MENTION THE "MOTOR NEWS" WHEN WRITING.

(49) 'No Hazards or Risks with A & B Taxies' – 1912
The most successful by far of the early taxi services was that provided by Messrs Wayte Brothers of Lemon Street, Off Grafton Street, Dublin. Reasonable charges, Speaking Tubes and 'careful drivers in uniform' all contributed to their success.
Source: RIAC Archive

(50 and 51) The Irish Depot of the Continental Tyre and Rubber Company – 1907
The Continental Rubber and Guttapercha Company of Hanover were amongst the largest rubber manufacturers in the world in 1907. Their 'Continental' brand of tyre was popular in Ireland and in that year they established a depot and offices at number 183 Great Brunswick Street, Dublin. Interestingly, repairs were sent to Britain and were guaranteed to be returned within three days.
Source: RIAC Archive

(52) W H Alexander & Company, Belfast – 1911

One of the best-known and longest established of Belfast's motor firms was W H Alexander & Company. Amongst the makes the company was an agent for was Enfield and this photograph shows a just delivered Enfield car with its proud new owner, a Mr T Sloan of Belfast.
Source: RIAC Archive

(53) Junior Army & Navy Stores Albion – 1911

A delivery van specially built on a 16 hp Albion chassis by the City Wheel and Carriage Works, Dublin, for the Junior Army & Navy Stores of D'Olier Street, Dublin.
Source: RIAC Archive

(54) A Dundalk 'Commer' – 1911

By 1911, buses had come into use between most Irish towns, and although the layout and design was becoming closer to what we are more used to, passengers and driver were still very exposed to the elements. A good example is this Commer bus which began operating in Dundalk in 1911.

'DEFERRED PAYMENT AVAILABLE'

Advertising is very often the mirror of its time and the motor advertisements of the period between 1907 and 1918 were no exception. To the student of motoring history they supply much useful and pertinent information that would perhaps have been unavailable elsewhere. They also provide a commentary on the time. A good example of this was the phrase *'Hire Purchase Available'* or the more common *'Deferred Payment Available'* which began to appear around this time and was an indicator to a perhaps often cash-strapped upper class that gentlemen's cars could be purchased, to borrow another phrase from a later era, on the *'never-never'*.

About half of all motoring advertisements appearing in the Irish motoring journal, the *Motor News*, were placed by the British-based manufacturers or agents of various makes of car. The majority of the balance were placed by the local Irish agent. Of the remainder, prominent Irish advertisers included Huttons, the famous Dublin coach builders, Chambers, the Belfast-based Irish car manufacturer and W F Peare, whose Waterford garage consistently advertised itself as *'The Home of Irish Motoring'*. Pim Brothers of Great George's Street, Dublin, the famous department store, was another consistent advertiser and it's advertisements portray an array of motoring clothing, particularly for chauffeurs, in which they seem to have specialised.

You're always safe on
'SHELL'
Spring, Summer, Autumn, Winter,
OBTAINABLE EVERYWHERE.
See that the can is sealed.

There are many success advertisements for *'End-to-end'* trials and such-like demonstrations of a particular manufacturers cars economy/speed/reliability. Success in the great Irish Automobile Club Reliability Trials was widely advertised and had a positive effect on a car-buying public far less cynical that today's. There are a great many advertisements from petrol suppliers and it is striking that only two of them, Shell and Pratts – which later became Esso – survive today. Petrol quality varied enormously in those years and the more reputable company's took steps to protect their product's integrity. A long-running series of advertisements was that of Shell informing purchasers 'IT MUST BE SEALED' referring to the practice of unscrupulous dealers refilling their red two-gallon cans with inferior petrol which was then sold as Shell. To counter this the Shell company introduced a system of securing it's cans with a lead seal.

Medical doctors remained the target of a lot of car advertising and indeed, testimonial advertisements featuring the experiences of doctors were much in evidence. One company who used this form of endorsement was the Belfast manufacturer, Chambers. Chambers was a prolific advertiser, a fact which today gives us much information about their range of cars and the differing models they produced.

Sir W. Goff's
35/45 h.p. Gladiator.

Mr. H. W. D. Goff's
18/28 h.p. Gladiator.

A few

GLADIATOR CARS

recently supplied to well known motorists in

IRELAND,

by

W. F. PEARE, GLADIATOR AGENT, WATERFORD.

The Marquess of Waterford's
35/45 h.p. Gladiator.

MODELS { BRITISH ... 18/24 h.p., 60 h.p. } From
{ FRENCH ... 12/14 to 35/45 h.p. } £325

CHAIN OR LIVE AXLE.

Full particulars of all from the above, or,

THE GLADIATOR CO.,

134 Long Acre, LONDON, W.

Mr. R. W. Morris's
18/24 h.p. Gladiator.

Mr. R. W. Keane's
14 18 h.p. Gladiator.

MENTION THE "MOTOR NEWS" WHEN WRITING.

(55) An advertisement for Gladiator Cars – 1908

The original Gladiator firm was founded in France in 1891 to make cycles and went through several changes of ownership during its lifetime. W F Peare of Waterford was an enthusiastic agent for Gladiator in Ireland and the make enjoyed a good reputation here. That reputation was, no doubt, helped by sales to such personages as The Marquis of Waterford and Sir W G D Goff, the Chairman of the Irish Automobile Club. For a brief time, certain of the company's models were made in Britain by the Austin company which explains the 'British' and 'French' models offered in this advertisement.
Source: RIAC Archive

Chauffeurs' Liveries.

We are giving special attention to this branch of our business.

———

Chauffeur's black leather jacket and breeches, **£2 : 12 : 6.**

———

Dark blue, green or brown livery jacket. Lancer shape front, lined tweed, sleeves and shoulders interlined waterproof cloth **£4 : 10 : 0.** Breeches, laced knees.

———

Oxford grey tweed livery jacket and breeches, **£2 : 12 : 0.**

———

Blue or brown drill overall suits, **6s. each.**

———

Illustrations and Prices free on application.

PIM BROS., Ltd., Sth. Gt. George's St., DUBLIN.

(56) What the well-dressed Chauffeur wore – 1907

By 1907, chauffeurs, as the automobile's reliability improved, had progressed from their early roles of puncture repair man and general mechanic to a role much closer to that with which we associate them today. As such it became important that they were dressed appropriately as befitted the status of their master or mistress. Pim Brothers of South Great George's Street, Dublin, were on hand to supply such needs to suit all situations.
Source: RIAC Archive

Chambers Motors Limited

CUBA STREET WORKS BELFAST.

UNSOLICITED TESTIMONIAL.

6 Church Street, Banbridge,
26/3/'08.

Gentlemen,

I have now had my 10 h.p. car (side entrance) a little over five months, and it has given me complete satisfaction. Since I got it I have done over 1,600 miles with absolutely no trouble and without a stop.

My petrol consumption, even with all my short journeys and frequent stoppages and startings, which run away with petrol and I always stop my engine when paying a visit works out at 29 miles to the gallon. The other day I did over 72 miles with four heavy men in the car on two gallons and a quart.

Since you delivered the car I have been continuously ploughing through mud and slush, but even so, how different my work is to pushing a cycle. But now since the roads have dried up driving is simply glorious, and the car just " skims " along, and only that you feel you are going you would almost fancy the car was stopped she is so silent and smooth running. Wishing you every success. Yours faithfully,

(Signed) R. MARTIN,
Medical Officer, Banbridge Dispensary District.

(57) A Doctor's Testimonial – 1908
The desirability of members of the Medical Profession driving their products led many motor manufacturers to advertise special 'Doctor's Models' as well as to use testimonials as to their success and reliability wherever possible. The Belfast manufacturer, Chambers, were no exception and this advertisement, with its testimonial by the Medical Officer of the Banbridge Dispensary District appeared widely during 1908. *Source: RIAC Archive*

TORPEDO BODIES.
SILENT 12-16.
ALL IRISH MANUFACTURE.
CHAMBERS MOTORS, Ltd.,
BELFAST.

(58) The Chambers 12/16 with Torpedo body – 1911
By 1911, Chambers Motors had concentrated their production on the 12/14 hp 4 cylinder silent-geared model which was usually fitted with a torpedo body. This proved to be one of Chambers most successful models and many testimonials were received from satisfied owners. One car was recorded as having covered 37,000 miles in a year and six months, averaging 500 miles per week.
Source: RIAC Archive

(59) Shell Motor Spirit 'Seals' – 1907

Initially, motor spirit was sold in chemist's shops, but this soon gave way to the ubiquitous two-gallon can which could be purchased at the first garages as well as from the many hotels who kept a stock for touring motorists. A deposit was paid for the safe return of the empty can and this led to unscrupulous dealers refilling them with inferior product. The result was the fitting of lead seals to genuine Shell cans (a practice also followed by Anglo-American, Shell's main competitor in Ireland). Shell Motor Spirit and its familiar red cans first became available throughout Ireland in 1904.

Source: RIAC Archive

THE PIONEERS OF HIGH-GRADE CARS AT LOW PRICES.

MITCHELL-LEWIS MOTOR CO.

(OF LONDON), LTD.

A WIDE RANGE OF MODELS.

DUBLIN AGENT—

A. O'NEILL & SON, 171 North Strand

A SUITABLE CAR FOR IRELAND.

Address
AGENCY APPLICATIONS.

MITCHELL-LEWIS MOTOR CO.
(OF LONDON), LTD.,

171 Great Portland Street,
LONDON.

Telegrams—" Mitlemocar."

1912 15-20 h.p. Mitchell Car, complete as shown, for £225.

(60) 'A Suitable Car for Ireland' – 1912
Many manufacturers advertised their cars as being ' a suitable car for Ireland'. In this case the offering is a Mitchell 15/20 hp car for £225. What made it suitable for Ireland is not, however, made apparent!
Source: RIAC Archive

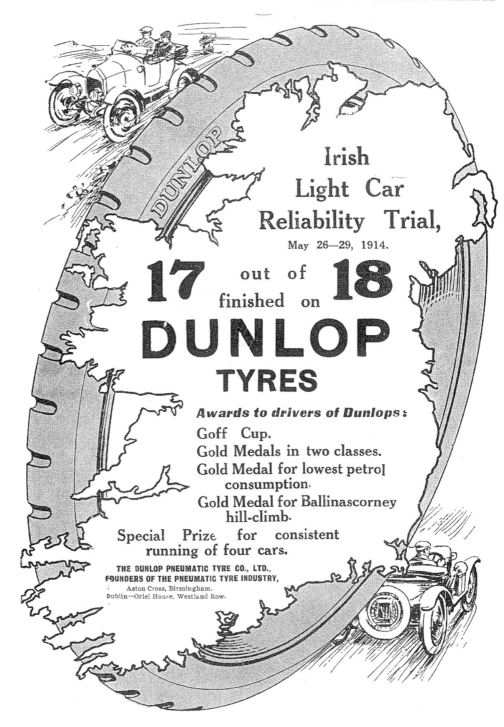

(61) Success in the Irish Light Car Reliability Trial – 1914

Not only the car manufacturers advertised their success in Irish Reliability Trials. So too did petrol suppliers, and in this case, the tyre companies. Dunlop, of course, manufactured pneumatic tyres at Oriel House, Westland Row, Dublin, a building which still survives today.
Source: RIAC Archive

(62) Sunlight Soap Leads the Way! – 1912
Not a specifically Irish advertisement, but one that appeared extensivly in Britain and
Ireland and which illustrates in an amusing way how much the motor car had become
a part of popular culture by 1912. Source: Author's Collection

PROMINENT MOTORISTS

The wealthy and famous took to the new past-time of motoring with gusto in the early years. Many prominent personalities were early car owners and this no doubt added to the growing appeal of the car. Irish society was no different and such notables as the First Earl of Iveagh; the Earl of Dudley, the Lord Lieutenant of Ireland; and Sir Horace Plunkett were all early and influential devotees of the car.

The car quickly became acceptable on the more formal occasions of the Irish social calendar and at the gatherings of society such as the Royal Dublin Horse Show, Leopardstown and Punchestown Horse races, polo matches in the Phoenix Park and week-end 'House' parties.

The purchase of a new car was an occasion and, happily for the motor historian, often a photograph of the owner and his new car was taken and circulated to the society magazines. In addition, some garages, or, as was sometimes the case, coach-builders, took photographs for their own records of each car supplied and it's often individual bodywork. Where they survive, these photographs today provide an invaluable record.

Cars also became a valid part of many formal photographs taken of some of the great family's of Ireland. It became usual to include a photograph of the owner's 'stud' of motor cars with his family and himself on and about them in front of the family residence and once again, many such photographs have come down to us. A good example in this chapter is the photograph of Sir Charles and Lady Barrington and family photographed at Glenstal, County Limerick in 1908.

(63) A Rolls–Royce in the Dublin Mountains – 1915

Oliver St. John Gogarty, surgeon, senator, playwright, poet and celebrated wit, was also a Rolls-Royce enthusiast. This photograph was taken on the road approaching Sally Gap and shows Gogarty at the wheel of his Rolls-Royce crossing what was reputed to be the first bridge over the River Liffey.
Source: RIAC Archive

(64) Lady Gregory and George Bernard Shaw at Coole House with Wolseley Laudellette – 1915

Lady Gregory and George Bernard Shaw look on as a small child tries the driving seat of a Wolseley Laudelette (*c.*1912). From the nursery window of Coole House more children look on. The photograph was probably taken at the end of Shaw's visit to Coole around mid-April 1915.
Source: RIAC Archive

(65) The Lord Lieutenant at the wheel of his Daimler leaving the Dublin Horse Show – 1907
The Lord Lieutenant of Ireland, Lord Aberdeen, at the wheel of his Daimler car leaving the 1907 Dublin Horse Show. Lord Grenfell, Commander-in-Chief of the Crown forces in Ireland is seated beside him.
Source: RIAC Archive

(66) Sir Charles and Lady Barrington & Family – 1908
Sir Charles and Lady Barrington and family photographed at Glenstal, County Limerick.
Source: RIAC Archive

(67) The House party at Powerscourt during Horse Show week – 1907
During the Dublin Horse Show, the House Party at Powerscourt was photographed with their cars outside the House. Those present were, from left: Lord and Lady Powerscourt; Lady Theresa Fitzwilliam; Lady Muriel Gore Brown, Countess of Kingstown; Miss Armitage; Captain Connolly; Captain Langrish; Hon W Trefusis; Hon. J Ashley; Colonel Gore Brown; Captain Beaumont; Captain Laverton and Mr and Mrs Beaumont Vestillo.
Source: RIAC Archive

(68) The Earl of Dunraven on his new Crossley – 1908
When this photograph was taken in February 1908, the Earl of Dunraven, who is pictured seated in his new 40 hp
Crossely car, was about to depart on a trip to Pau in France. The Crossley was described as '*one of the most handsome
vehicles ever turned out by the firm. It is finished in a fine pale grey, the mouldings of the carriage body being brought into relief by
the addition of light red lines. The carriage body is upholstered in pale grey morocco leather, and all the fittings are in nickel silver.
The general lines of the carriage body are exceptionally neat*'. Lord Dunraven, it was also noted '*always makes a point of
driving himself on his long motor expeditions.*'
Source: *RIAC Archive*

**(69) Lady Maurice
Fitzgerald's 14/20
Siddeley – 1908**
Taken at Lady Fitzgerald's
residence, Johnstown Castle,
Wexford, this is a fine 14/20
hp Siddeley. The car was
supplied by Messrs
Thompson Brothers of
Wexford and was used
extensively for touring in
Counties Kerry and Galway.
Source: *RIAC Archive*

(70) The Hon. Miss O'Brien on her Argyll car – 1909
The Hon. Miss O'Brien on her Argyll car. In the tonneau are Lady
O'Brien and Miss Ellen O'Brien. Miss O'Brien was the daughter of
the Lord Chief Justice of Ireland and was a noted and ardent
huntswoman. *Source: RIAC Archive*

**(71) The Misses Bobbett of Leixlip entering their Napier
– 1911**
The Misses Bobbett of Leixlip, County Kildare, entering their Napier
car in which they are about to set out to make an afternoon call.
Source: RIAC Archive

(72) Sir Horace Plunkett on his Daimler car – 1909
Sir Horace Plunkett, founder of the Co-Operative movement and at the time this
photograph was taken in 1909, Vice-President of the Irish Automobile Club, on his new
Daimler car. The photograph was taken outside his beloved Kilteragh, which was burnt by
Irregulars in 1923. *Source: RIAC Archive*

(73) The Daimler presented to John Redmond – 1912
In 1912, a 25 hp Daimler was purchased by public subscription and was presented to John Redmond, Chairman of the Irish Parliamentary Party. The special Landaulette body was built by Messrs Huttons, the famous coach builders of Summerhill, Dublin.
Source: RIAC Archive

(74) Stanley Cochrane's Rolls-Royce – 1914
This magnificent Rolls-Royce was supplied to Stanley Cochrane by Messrs. J B Ferguson of Baggot Street, Dublin, in whose works the body was built.
Source: RIAC Archive

(75) The Chairman of the Irish Automobile Club – *c.* 1907
Sir William G D Goff was the greatly-respected and influential chairman of the Irish Automobile Club in its founding years. A noted cyclist and later a pioneer motorist, he took part in all the events of the Irish Automobile Club's early years. He is pictured at the wheel of a Gladiator with, in the back seat, W F Peare, the agent for the make, and in the front passenger seat, his chauffeur, Milne.
Source: RIAC Archive

ROADS AND MOTOR TOURISM

Roads, or rather the lack of anything that could reasonably be described as a road, were a matter of ongoing concern to the Irish motorist. It is not insignificant that John S Brown, who imported the first car into Ireland in March 1896, next set about founding the Irish Roads Improvement Association. For many years landowners and the public authorities had neglected their responsibilities to maintain in good order the roads which passed through their areas.

The arrival of the car and its subsequent rapid growth in numbers in the first two decades of the twentieth century put enormous pressure on the road system here. It has to be said that it was the car-owners themselves who banded together in Road Improvement groups and who lobbied for the much-needed improvements. Several important Road Congress gatherings were held where the best type of road surface and building materials were discussed at length and in surprising detail. The use of steam-rollers was much discussed and debated and it was held to be a national scandal by car users that in 1910 there were only three local authorities in the whole of Ireland employing steam rollers for the improvement of their roads.

Things did improve slowly, however, but despite this many roads remained appalling and were turned into a sticky, muddy mess by rain – a condition with which we have more than a nodding acquaintance in Ireland. In dry weather, dust was the great enemy and various 'dust-sealing' inventions were tried and, alas, all found wanting.

The development of motor tourism which had begun to grow due to the ongoing efforts of R J Mecredy was severely hampered by this deficit in the condition of our roads. Mecredy was himself directly instrumental in having the Killarney to Kenmare road surfaced and made suitable for tourist traffic, with great resultant benefit to the local hoteliers and to the opening up of this area of great natural beauty to tourism. Mecredy's maps, including his special *'Mecredy's Steam-rolled Road Map of Ireland'*, were much relied upon.

Mecredy's Maps were widely in use at this time by all road users and gave an accurate indication of the sort of road conditions a motorist could expect to encounter by means of a coloured grading system. Even after Irish roads had greatly improved, Mecredy's Maps continued to be the standard map used by the majority of Irish motorists.

(76) Off the beaten track – a touring Sheffield-Simplex – 1915
Although the location of this photograph cannot be identified, it serves to show how bad many Irish roads were in 1915. These road conditions were by no means exceptional and one can only imagine what they were like after rain. The 30 hp Sheffield-Simplex was a beautifully-built, modern but quite conventional car.
Source: RIAC Archive

(77) The suspension bridge across the Kenmare River – 1915
The suspension bridge over the Kenmare River on the road from Glengarrif to Kenmare was a well-known feature of the locality, Here a bus is about to cross the bridge with a party of tourists.
Source: RIAC Archive

(78) Ireland's only Prohibition Post – 1908
Uniquely, Ireland had only one road officially closed to motor traffic. The road which acquired this distinction
was the coast road from Portmarnock to Malahide in County Dublin. The County Council sought permission to
close the road owing to its dangerous nature running alongside cliffs overlooking the sea. Permission was granted
and the required prohibition sign was erected at both ends of the road.
Source: RIAC Archive

(79) Dr Charles Blood of Limerick and his 18 hp De Dion – 1908
The *Motor News* carried this photograph of Dr and Mrs Charles Blood and their new 18 hp four-cylinder De
Dion car at the end of 1908. The magazine reported: '*Dr Blood is most enthusiastic regarding its noiselessness and
smoothness of running. This speaks well for the car's durability, for the roads in County Limerick and the adjacent County
Clare are the worst in Ireland.*' Dr Blood was quoted as saying '*We have done a great deal of touring this past Summer
and Autumn and of all my experiences at home and abroad I have never seen such bad roads as there are in Limerick and
Clare, and I warn motorists to avoid all the main roads in these two counties, as the vibration over utterly neglected roads is
ruinous to one's car and temper.*'
Source: RIAC Archive

(80) Tarvia spraying vehicle in Phoenix Park – 1909

Dust on Irish roads continued to be a major problem for motorists and other road users right up into the 1930s. Many ingenious attempts to cure the 'dust' problem were tried with varying degrees of success. 'Tarvia' was a tar preparation from which all water, ammonical liquor and the lighter volatile oils had been removed by distillation. Manufactured in Ireland by the Dublin Tar company, this photograph of a Tarvia spraying vehicle was taken while trials were being carried out along the main road of Dublin's Phoenix Park.

Source: RIAC Archive

(81) Irish Tourist Development Syndicate's motor Chars-a-banc – 1911

The Commer chars-a-banc of the Tourist Development Syndicate Limited photographed at Windy Gap, where the roads connecting Killarney, Sneem and Kenmare meet. Two of the cars were *en route* from Parknasilla to Killarney and another from Killarney to Kenmare. The famous Gap of Dunloe is visible in the background where the light is streaming through a triangular opening in the Magillicuddy Reeks.

Source: RIAC Archive

(82) H S Huet's Royal Starling car at Newtownmountkennedy – 1908

The Royal Starling car of H S Huet was photographed driving through the village of Newtownmountkennedy on the way to the Irish Automobile Club's Ballinaslaughter hillclimb in 1908. The Royal Starling was manufactured by the Star Engineering Company of Wolverhampton, and H S Huet was their Irish representative.

Source: RIAC Archive

(83) Commer Char-a-banc at the Royal Hotel, Glendalough – 1912
The Dublin firm of Messrs. Thompson's operated a very popular excursion service from Dublin to Glendalough in the Wicklow Mountains using a large Commer char-a-banc. So popular did this service become that Thompson's were soon obliged to acquire a second Commer char-a-banc. The photograph shows one of the chars-a-banc arriving with a full compliment of passengers at the Royal Hotel, Glendalough.
Source: RIAC Archive

(84) Mecredy's Steam-rolled Road Map of Ireland – 1912
The Irish road authorities were slow to undertake the work necessary to upgrade their roads to make them suitable for motorised transport. Even as late as 1912, steam-rollers and the steam rolling of roads was comparatively rare. The enterprising Mecredy Percy & Company produced this map showing which roads were steam-rolled. Deservedly, it became a best-seller. *Source: RIAC Archive*

(85) Heading for the North – 1917
A Stellite car on the road to Belfast, passing The Cock Inn between Balbriggan and Drogheda. The Stellite was made by a subsidiary of Wolseley, the Electric and Ordnance Accessories Company of Birmingham. It was an 1,100 cc economy car and ceased production in 1919 to make way for Wolseley's own ohc Ten.
Source: RIAC Archive

(86) On the Naas Road – 1917
On the Naas Road, at the Dew Drop Inn, a fully loaded car passes another whose occupants have retired to the Inn for refreshment. Such Inns proliferated the roads of Ireland at this time. Sadly, the majority have now disappeared.
Source: RIAC Archive

(87) The disappearing Toll-house – 1915
In the early part of the twentieth century, the once familiar toll-houses of the previous century began to rapidly disappear as roads were improved. Happially, this particular toll-house is one of the few that has survived to this day and is situated at Kilmoon, north of Ashbourne, on the Ashbourne to Slane road. *Source: RIAC Archive*

(88) A Rover sidecar entering the woods at Glendhu – 1915
The Great War greatly increased the popularity of motorcycles as an economical and convenient means of transport. The addition of a sidecar to a motorcycle further increased their convenience and versatility and provided a means of enjoying the freedom of the road for many who could not afford a car. This Rover motorcycle and sidecar were photographed entering the woods at Glendu in County Wicklow. *Source: RIAC Archive*

THE DREADED 'SIDE SLIP'

If there was one subject which preoccupied the minds of early motorists it was the dreaded 'side-slip'. This was the name given to what we would today call a skid – usually on slippery or changing surfaces. The sudden resultant loss of control was not understood by motorists and how it should be dealt with was the subject of all sorts of, to our ears at least, strange theories.

As a result of this in-built dread in most motorist's minds, many accidents attributable to other factors were mistakenly blamed on the 'side-slip' with the result that fear of it grew until it became like an invisible monster silently stalking every motorist.

Motorists, did however, fact many other hazards on our roads apart from the skid. The fact that most roads had a loose surface led to a constant danger of blow-outs on tyres that were very vulnerable to puncture when compared to their modern counterparts. And when it rained, road surfaces could quickly change to a sticky, muddy mess that made progress slow, not to mention dangerous. Many roads had deep drainage channels running either side of them and the unmade surface assisted their crumbling along the edges as the weight of a car passed over, with a slide into the ditch resulting in perhaps, if one was lucky, just a broken wheel or two.

Many roads were very narrow, providing just enough width for the passage of a single vehicle so that when two cars met along such a road, one usually had to back-up, often for a considerable distance. Sometimes, one would attempt to turn around, with the result shown in this chapter.

Brake failure was yet another hazard faced by the motorist of this period. Mechanically actuated brakes were vulnerable to wear and tear and it was not uncommon to hear of 'runaway' cars and buses. Brakes, not particularly efficient at the best of times, often only acting on the rear wheels, could disappear and the motorist who could bring his vehicle to a safe stop after such a failure was regarded as something of a hero.

One final hazard which it is perhaps particularly appropriate to mention as we draw near to the re-introduction of a tram service in Dublin, is the danger occasioned by the passage of these vehicles on roads shared by cars and other vehicles. It was not uncommon for cars to become caught between trams with the result one can see later in this chapter. Dublin motorists, take heed, you have been warned!

(89) An upturned car in Dublin's Phoenix Park – 1912
The deceptively tight double bends between the Magazine Fort and St Mary's Hospital (then the Hibernian Military School) in the Phoenix Park caught out the chauffeur of this Daimler limousine who was driving its owner, County Court Judge Todd, at the time. Little damage was done other than a bent front axle and the Huttons breakdown gang are shown arriving in the background of the photograph. *Source: RIAC Archive*

(90) The Danger of Water Channels – 1909
The car shown in this photograph met with an accident on the narrow road between Laragh and Glendalough. The near side wheels slipped into the deep water channel at the side of the road, and in attempting to get the car out, the back wheel collapsed. Such unprotected, deep water channels were common alongside Irish roads. *Source: RIAC Archive*

(91) A 'smashed' car – 1909
This Daimler, the property of Lord de Clifford, after it had left the road apparently at speed, ended up in a field. Although the car was badly smashed, the occupants escaped with minor cuts and scrapes.
Source: RIAC Archive

(92) An Accident on the Bray Road – 1909
This accident occurred on the Bray Road at Loughlinstown Hill. The car overturned and one passenger was pinned beneath it. The car was lifted sufficiently to free him and he was brought to the nearby workhouse infirmary. A crowd of onlookers having gathered, it was then suggested that the car should be righted and moved to the side of the road as it was blocking other vehicles passage. Many willing hands quickly righted the car but in the process the uninjured driver somehow managed to end up under the car! Now injured, he too was removed to the infirmary.
Source: RIAC Archive

(93) Nearly a smash – 1912
A motor lorry of Messrs W and R Jacob and Company which got out of control in Westmoreland Street, Dublin, happily without injury to anyone. Perhaps, wet cobblestones had a bearing on the incident?
Source: RIAC Archive

(94 and 95) A Runaway Bus – *c.* 1909
The Dunmore East to Waterford bus service vehicle
is shown in these two photographs – in one of
which we can see the result of it '*running away down
Leopardstown Hill while coming from Dunmore East to
Waterford.*'
Source: RIAC Archive

(96) A bad 'Side-slip' on the Merrion Road – 1915
This Renault was travelling along the Merrion Road, Dublin, when it skidded, turning around completely and going up on to the footpath. It then swung round again just missing the tram pole visible in the photograph. Most of the damage seems to have been confined to the rear wheel and one surmises that the occupants were fortunate to avoid hitting another vehicle. One's chances of surviving a similar manoeuvre on this busy road without hitting another vehicle today would be almost certainly zero. *Source: RIAC Archive*

(97) Don't fall asleep at the Wheel! – 1915
The driver of this 15.9 Swift fell asleep while driving in County Armagh. The Swift left the road and demolished a stone wall, overturning in the process. The driver was lucky to escape relatively uninjured and the car stood up surprisingly well to it's drivers misadventure.
Source: RIAC Archive

(98) A near thing on a Limerick Bridge – 1915
This Daimler lorry belonging to Messrs J N Russell and Company struck the parapet of a bridge at Limerick. Despite the damage done to the bridge, the lorry seems to have escaped relatively unscathed. The driver attributed the accident to a 'side-slip'.
Source: RIAC Archive

(99) The Pitfalls of Glenmalure – 1915

A common complaint by Irish motorists was the lack of passing places on mountain or remote roads. When two vehicles met on such a road, one had no choice but to back up, often a considerable distance. In this photograph taken at Glenmalure, the car attempted to turn around on the narrow road, almost inevitably sliding into the ditch, from which strenuous efforts are being made to rescue it.

Source: RIAC Archive

(100) The result of being caught between two Trams – 1915
The owner of this Morris-Oxford attempted to overtake a tram when another was approaching in the opposite direction. With the imminent arrival of the 'Luas' light rail tram system in Dublin, perhaps motorists should take note of a new hazard.
Source: RIAC Archive

(101) The combined result of a swerve and a burst Tyre – 1915
Mr A C Houlihan, a Roscrea solicitor, was driving this Sunbeam with four passengers when a woman with a donkey suddenly pulled across in front of him. As a result of his sudden swerve to avoid her a tyre burst and the car left the road, going through a low hedge, dropping down a distance of about six feet into a field.
Source: RIAC Archive

(102) A Ford Service Van – 1917
As cars proliferated, it didn't take long for breakdown vans to be designed and employed to deal with their mishaps. This Ford Service Van was operated by Autocars of Grathan Street, Dublin. No doubt it was kept busy.
Source: RIAC Archive

THE IAC
IRISH RELIABILITY TRIALS

First held in 1906, the IAC Reliability Trials were the great Irish motor sporting events of this period. Teams of cars entered by the major manufacturers of the day vied with each other to capture the various prizes but the real reward was to be able to advertise success in this event. In that less cynical age the endorsement of a win in the Irish event was directly translatable into sales by the manufacturer.

Successes were widely advertised and the Irish and Scottish Reliability Trials were regarded as the sternest possible test of a motorcar by the public of Britain and Ireland. Small wonder then that in the weeks leading up to the Irish event in either May or June the streets of Dublin buzzed with the activities of the 'works' teams assembling for the event. Cars were tested, publicity photographs were taken, fuel consumption calculations were carried out and the level of activity around the clubhouse of the organising club, the Irish Automobile Club, was such as to make it impossible for most of the better-off citizenry of Dublin not to be aware of the upcoming event. And when at last the first day of the event dawned, crowds gathered in Dawson Street to witness the cars and their crews – each one was obliged to carry a club observer – issue forth from the Club Garage where they had assembled.

Repairs en route – Every minute loses a mark!

The route itself could be relied upon to test severely all the competitors and their cars. Lasting between four and six days, it was not uncommon for the competitors to traverse from Dublin to one end of the island and then to the other end followed by a circuit of some of the toughest roads in Kerry before returning to Dublin for the finish. Usually there were several speed trials along the route together with a number of hillclimbs, Holywood and Ballinaslaughter, being particular favourites of the organisers. Those that had run 'non-stop', that is to say without a forced stop because of a mechanical problem, and who had been reasonably fast on the speed elements, could have an expectation of an award and all that would go with that.

However, the real winners in these events were the public for the Irish Reliability Trials made a very real and positive contribution to the development of the motor car and to the continuing quest for greater reliability in its day-to-day use.

The years between 1906 and 1909 were the great years of the Irish Reliability Trials and although the event was revived as a Light Car Reliability Trial in 1914, entries were far fewer than in the earlier years and the event didn't regain its importance.

(103) 15 hp Ford Junior in the 1907 Trials

Ford cars had just been introduced to Ireland and were regarded by the press as '*too spidery for Irish conditions.*' An early advocate of the make was R J Mecredy, editor of the *Motor News*. Trials such as the 1907 event were to convince many of the Ford's abilities.

Source: RIAC Archive

(104) The Humber Team – 1907

The Humber team in the 1907 Irish Automobile Club's Irish Reliability Trial photographed outside the premises of their Dublin agent, Keating's Motor Works.

Source: RIAC Archive

(105) Getting on to Magilligan Strand for the Speed Test – 1907
The Irish Automobile Club arranged for boards to be laid down to enable the competitor's cars to get to the Strand without difficulty. Here, Captain Lindsay Knox's Orleans is leading the way along the boards.
Source: RIAC Archive

(106) J B Greake's 15 hp De Dion being 'assisted' – 1907
Getting on to the strand at Magilligan proved more difficult for some. This is the 15 hp De Dion of J B Greake being 'assisted' onto the course.
Source: RIAC Archive

(107) A 15/20 hp Clement-Talbot ascending the hill at Holywood – 1907
The Clement Talbot of H D Day, which ran non-stop for four days, ascending the hill at Holywood during the speed trial there.
Source: RIAC Archive

(108) Luncheon at Abbeyleix – 1907
The competitors cars at Abbeyleix during the luncheon interval on the last day of the Trials. Luncheon was supplied by 'Hum' Bland, who lived nearby, and was a leading organiser in several of the Irish Automobile Club Reliability Trials.
Source: RIAC Archive

(109) Harvey du Cros Jnr. and Willie du Cros – 1907
Harvey du Cros Jnr. and Willie du Cros photographed on the Austin cars they drove in the Trials. The Austin of Harvey du Cros ran non-stop for the four days of the Trials while that of Willie du Cros ran for three days non-stop following a one minute stop on the first day's run. *Source: RIAC Archive*

(110) T W Murphy in his 8 hp Rover on the Weighbridge – 1908
As well as being checked for safety and eligibility for their class, competitors cars were weighed before the start. This is the 8 hp Rover of T W Murphy photographed on the weighbridge. A founder member of the Motor Cycle Union of Ireland and a pioneer motorcyclist and motorist, T W Murphy was on the staff of both the *Irish Cyclist* and the *Motor News*. A keen competitor, he was twice winner of the Ariel Cup for the Two-Hundred Miles Non-stop Motor Cycle Trial in 1904 and 1905. After the demise of these two publications he wrote for the *Irish Times* and many other publications, becoming the 'grand old man of Irish motor sport' until his death in 1953.
Source: RIAC Archive

(111) Body measuring at Ballsbridge – 1908
Before starting the event, competitors cars were examined to ensure that they were eligible for the class in which they were entered. In this photograph the Irish Automobile Club officials are checking that the declared body type is within its allowed dimensions.
Source: RIAC Archive

(112) A 10/12 hp Humber on Holywood Hill – 1908
The 10/12 hp Humber which made fastest time in its class driven by G Phillips photographed during its ascent of Holywood Hill. *Source: RIAC Archive*

(113) Assisting a Minerva. – 1908
The 28 hp Minerva driven by P Robinson which got into difficulty and sank in soft ground while avoiding other traffic. As can be seen, ample numbers were on hand to assist it to regain the road.
Source: RIAC Archive

(114) Officials and Competitors – 1908
The Officials (centre front) and Competitors at the Southern Hotel, Killarney. *Source: RIAC Archive*

(115) The tunnel on the Kenmare Road – 1908
The 60 hp Napier driven by F G Cundy entering the tunnel on the Kenmare Road.
Source: RIAC Archive

(116) A Daimler in trouble – 1908
The 48 hp Daimler driven by T L Plunkett had an adventurous Trial. On the first day it was in collision with an artillery wagon, while on the second day it skidded, broke a wheel and overturned. Luckily, its driver and passengers escaped with only minor injuries.
Source: RIAC Archive

(117) Overtaking on Ballinaslaughter Hillclimb – 1908
The 20 hp Sunbeam of F Eastmead overtakes the 10/12 hp Chambers
of J Hurst (No 25) on Ballinaslaughter Hillclimb.
Source: RIAC Archive

(118) W G Wilkinson's 15 hp Rover on Farmer's Hill – 1909
The 15 hp Rover of W G Wilkinson in full flight in Farmer's Hill at
Tralee, County Kerry. It will be noted that the fowl are also in full
flight. *Source: RIAC Archive*

(119) Emerging from the tunnel on the Kenmare to Killarney Road – 1909
The tunnel on the Kenmare to Killarney road was a well-known feature of the area and is here a backdrop to the emerging 12 hp Humber of G A Philips. *Source: RIAC Archive*

(120) The Limerick Luncheon Stop – 1909
Competitors cars at rest in Limerick's George Street during the luncheon stop on the third day of the Trials.
Source: RIAC Archive

(121) The Official Humber – 1909
H G Day's Talbot car passing the Official Humber at one of the events many Controls.
Source: RIAC Archive

(122) On Grennan Hillclimb – 1909
A 15 hp Marlborough at speed on the Greenan Hill, near Londonderry. *Source: RIAC Archive*

LOST MAKES

To the student of motoring history, the list of car manufacturers that existed in the years up to the Great War is a source of endless fascination. G R Doyle, the author of the classic work, *The World's Automobiles*, calculated that in 1932 there were no fewer than 2,134 manufacturers in production! By the time a new edition of his work appeared in 1957 that listing had grown to 3,913 for the same period while he calculated that only 500 were then still in production. It is safe to assume that in the period with which this book is concerned, 1907-1918, this figure was very considerably higher than 2,134 and probably nearer to 3,000.

So, what became of this vast proliferation of car manufacturers? Many only existed for a short time in the heady days of the car's first flowering. Some never got beyond the production of a few prototypes, but the greatest number fell victim to the harsh economic winds that prevailed after the Great War. Many had turned their production to the manufacture under contract of munitions or aircraft during the conflict and were forced out of car production so that they might survive the tardy repayment for this work afterwards. Forced to invest in plant and machinery to meet this wartime need, once the conflict had ended they simply could not sustain their increased overheads while awaiting payment for their war-time work.

Amongst the many that failed were some who deserved to succeed. Several of these are portrayed in this chapter and it is striking how some makes were particularly popular in the years leading up to 1914, in contrast to the makes that succeeded after the conflict. Some perished on peculiarities of their design which in the evolutionary onrush in the design of the motor car then taking place, they failed to appreciate were no longer what the public wanted. Some were simply over ambitious and learned that enthusiasm is never a substitute for proper financing. Still more simply failed to make any significant impact on their intended market at a time when word-of-mouth was the best advertising one could have.

There were but a handful of Irish attempts to start manufacture, and these have already been detailed in an earlier chapter. Even allowing for the lack of an infrastructure of light engineering firms anywhere other than around the ship-building city of Belfast, this seems extraordinary. Perhaps, we Irish, with but a few notable exceptions, lacked the self-belief to begin such ventures at that time.

(123) The West-Aster of Lord Powerscourt – 1907

This magnificent 22 hp West-Aster was purchased by Lord Powerscourt in 1907 and initially proved to be quite troublesome. However, its various problems were sorted out one by one and the West-Aster became in time a reliable and much admired car. E J West had previously made the Progress car, and there was little difference between the first West's and the last Progress. By 1908 West offered a range of cars from 10/12 hp to 35 hp but went into receivership in May 1908 and ceased production.
Source: RIAC Archive

(124) Four White Steam cars – c. 1907

Four White Steam cars photographed in County Wicklow about 1907. The drivers are, from left to right: Lord Louth, Stanley Cochrane, Dr J Colohan and an unidentified motorist. Robert H White of the White Sewing Machine Company in Cleveland produced his first steam car in 1900. Whites gained a good reputation in trials and reached the height of their popularity when the American President, Theodore Roosevelt, used a White during his presidency. White continued to offer steam cars until 1911 when they began to offer petrol-engined cars. By 1918 production of cars ceased as the company had shifted its attention to trucks.
Source: RIAC Archive

(125) The Deasy 1,000 mile Trial – 1907

Another make using a Trial to publicise their product was Deasy which carried out a 1,000 mile journey around Ireland in March and April 1907. The Deasy is seen setting out from the Clubhouse of the Irish Automobile Club at the start of its run. Deasy cars were manufactured in Coventry from 1906 to 1911. Sponsored by an Irishman, Captain H P Deasy, the original Deasy car was a 4 1/2 litre 4-cylinder model with several unusual features. These included a side-valve monobloc power unit, transverse rear suspension, pressure lubrication and both sets of brakes working on huge drums on the rear wheels.
Source: RIAC Archive

(126) Mr and Mrs A J Wilson in their 22 hp Minerva – 1907

The Belgian De Jong brothers began to manufacture Minerva cars in 1900, remaining in production until 1939. A J Wilson – famous as the cyclist 'Faed' – was an ardent supporter of the make and is pictured here with his wife, daughter and niece in his 22 hp Minerva in 1907. Minervas were popular with Irish motorists, many of whom would no doubt have agreed with Wilson's assessment that *'There are more luxurious cars, faster cars, more flexible cars; but, at its price, I am very satisfied that the Minerva is hard to beat.'*
Source: RIAC Archive

(127) A Calcott car at Glendalough – 1915

F A Wallen, a well-known Dublin motor agent for Calcott cars photographed beside the Upper Lake at Glendalough. The 10 hp Calcott provided roomy, reliable transport at a modest price. Calcott Bros. Limited, which manufactured its cars at Coventry, was acquired by Singer in 1926.
Source: RIAC Archive

(128) A Darracq beside the World's Largest Ship – 1914

A 16 hp Darracq offered for sale by Messrs. Harry Ferguson and photographed by the stern of the '*Britannic*' in the shipyard of Messrs. Harland and Wolff at Belfast. When completed, the 'Britannic' was the largest ship in the world. The Société A Darracq first began manufacturing cars as early as 1896. In various forms it proved to be one of the great surviours of the early motor industry and continued until 1959.
Source: RIAC Archive

(129) James Adam on his 20 hp Ariel – 1909

Mr James Adam of Holywell, Palmerstown Park, with his son and chauffeur on his 20 hp Ariel de Luxe photographed in 1909. Ariel began the manufacture of quads and tricycles at Birmingham in 1898 and produced their first car in 1902. A well-regarded make, they concentrated on motorcycles after the Great War but an unsuccessful foray into the booming small car market in 1923 brought about the end of the company in 1925.
Source: RIAC Archive

SPEED, HILLCLIMBS AND GYMKHANAS

In the earliest days of the car, motoring was seen as a sporting past-time by those with the means to indulge themselves in this new pursuit. As such it ranked with hunting, shooting and boating. As the car proliferated and other uses for it became more apparent this vision of the car changed and so too, did its sporting aspect. Sporting motoring competition is almost as old as the car itself and the first organised competition in Ireland for motor vehicles – in this case motorcycles – is generally regarded to have been a race run at the Navan horse racing course in August 1900.

The new Irish Auto-mobile Club was estab-lished in 1901 and began to organise competitive events as well as Tours which tested the ability of the car to travel reliably over some of the more remote parts of Ireland. The Gordon Bennett Race of 1903 is usually credited as being the event which made the Irish public 'car-conscious' for the first time and certainly it gave an added and important impetus to the growth of motor sport in Ireland. By then Ireland's pioneer racing driver, Leslie Porter, had competed, with tragic results, in the famous Paris to Madrid Race of 1903. Irish-born Moore-Brabazon won the 1907 Circuit des Ardennes in Belgium and the Guinness brothers, Algernon and Kenelm Lee, were carving out a name for themselves in Ireland and abroad.

Porter and Harry Robinson competed with distinction in the 1908 Tourist Trophy Race, the famous 'Four-Inch' Race, in the Isle of Man. Meanwhile the Irish Automobile Club had begun in 1906 the famous series of Reliability Trials which were amongst the most important events held in these islands up to the start of the Great War in 1914. But it was Kenelm Lee Guinness who became the first Irish driver to win a major international event when he was victorious driving a Sunbeam in the 1914 Tourist Trophy Race. This was so nearly a double triumph for the Guinness brothers, for Algernon held second place for most of the race only to retire with mechanical problems.

At home, apart from reliability Trials, hillclimbs such as the annual Ballinaslaughter event in County Wicklow vied for popularity with 'motor gymkhanas' catering for the perhaps less competitive motorist. Speed trials were also popular, held at such venues as Portmarnock's 'Velvet Strand', Magalligan and Rosslare Strands.

(130) S T Robinson at Ballinaslaughter Hillclimb – 1908

The Irish Automobile Clubs Hillclimb at Ballinaslaughter in County Wicklow was always a well supported event. In this photograph taken during the running of the 1908 event, S T Robinson's 15 hp Clement-Talbot is seen passing the fork on the course while on its way to winning the Henshaw Cup.

S T Robinson was a well-known competitor and motor engineer with premises at No. 27 South King Street, Dublin.

Source: RIAC Archive

(131) Harry Robinson at the wheel of his Calthorpe Racing Car – 1908

The Tourist Trophy Race in the Isle of Man had amongst its entry two Irishmen in the 1908 event – the famous 'Four-Inch' race. Both were driving Calthorpe cars for the factory. The drivers involved were Leslie Porter (who would finish a magnificent fourth against much faster machinery) and a young Dubliner, Harry Robinson. In the race, young Harry Robinson retired having overturned his Calthorpe.

Source: RIAC Archive

(132) Harry Robinson's Calthorpe starting in the 1908 TT

Harry Robinson starting the 1908 Tourist Trophy Race in his Calthorpe. The starter is Julian Orde of the Royal Automobile Club.

Source: RIAC Archive

(133) Dr W D Donnan at the wheel of his 10/12 hp Darracq – 1909

For several years the Royal North of Ireland Yacht Club held an annual hillclimb at Cultra, on the shores of Belfast Lough, and on the site of what is today the fine Ulster Folk and Transport Museum. This well-supported event attracted a fine selection of machinery and our photograph shows Dr W D Donnan ascending the hill at the wheel of his 10/12 hp Darracq, in which he placed seventh in his class.

Source: RIAC Archive

(134) Dublin & District Motor Cycle Club Easter Trial – 1916
Members of the Dublin & District Motor Cycle Club photographed at the luncheon break during their Easter Trial in 1916 at Woodenbridge, County Wicklow. Motor cycle competitions became very popular from the middle of the first decade of the twentieth century and were given further impetus by the dramatic growth in motor cycling's popularity during the Great War.
Source: RIAC Archive

(135) S T Robinson at the Rosslare Speed Trials – 1913
S T Robinson, having just set a time of 107 mph at the Speed Trials on Rosslare Strand, explains to Walter Sexton and Edward White of the Irish Automobile Club, why the course is no longer fit for racing.
Source: RIAC Archive

(136) A 10 hp AC Lightcar driven by 'Miss Nomer' – 1915
A 10 hp AC lightcar, driven by the anonymous 'Miss Nomer', took part in the reliability trial of the Dublin & District Motor Cycle Club to Glendalough and back on St. Patrick's Day 1915. The photograph shows 'Miss Nomer' setting out from the start. *Source: RIAC Archive*

(137) A R Wayte's 8 hp Morgan – 1915
Another competitor on the St. Patrick's Day event to Glendalough was this interesting early three-wheeler 8 hp Morgan. Driven by A R Wayte, the Morgan achieved a bronze medal. It was photographed at the control on the top of the Sugarloaf Hill. The first production Morgan appeared in 1911 and the marque quickly achieved sporting success. This is most probably a Sporting 1912 model.
Source: RIAC Archive

(138) Dublin & District Motor Cycle Club Portmarnock Speed Trials – 1912

A popular annual event was the Dublin & District Cycle Club's Speed Trials at Portmarnock's 'Velvet Strand'. Here are seen the cars of some of the many spectators who travelled to the venue. The 'Prohibition Road' described in an earlier chapter of this book began about one hundred yards further along this road towards Malahide. *Source: RIAC Archive*

(139) A Motor Gymkhana at Sion Mills – 1907

Motor Gymkhana's were intended as 'fun' events for less competitive motorists and were very popular at this time. Competitons at the Sion Mills Gymkhana included a Fancy Dress Race, a Backward Race, Musical Chairs and a Tortoise Race. *Source: RIAC Archive*

(140) The Successful Calthorpe Team in the Coupe des Voiturettes at Boulogne – 1909

Leslie Porter (centre) was part of the successful Calthorpe team which won the Regularity Cup in the Coupe des Boulogne in France in 1909. Their success was repeated in 1910. *Source: RIAC Archive*

141) The First Great Win by an Irishman in an International Motor Race – 1914

Kenelm Lee Guinness swings his Sunbeam through Hillberry Corner during his famous drive to victory in the 1914 Tourist Trophy Race on the Isle of Man. This was so nearly a double triumph for the Guinness brothers for Kenelm's brother Algernon, held second place before retiring late in the race.

Source: RIAC Archive

(142 and 143)
Irish drivers at the Circuit des Ardennes – 1907
This once classic Belgian race had by 1907 become a shadow of its former self. Nevertheless, it continued to be a prestigious and hard-fought event. In the 1907 race, Algernon Guinness and Moore-Brabazon drove Minerva cars into third and first places respectively in the first day's contest for the Coupe de l'Empereur.
Source: RIAC Archive.

THE AUTOMOBILE
GOES TO WAR

No other event in the early history of motoring gave such an impetus to the development of motoring as the Great War between 1914 and 1918. The military requirements of the warring nations led to a concentrated development of both chassis and engine so that in this short five year period, the reliability and performance of the motor car improved out of proportion to all of the years that had gone before.

Many were exposed to motor vehicles for the first time in the armed services. Many more learned to ride a motorcycle or drive a car and at the war's ending it was these people who stimulated the tremendous growth that occurred in motor car ownership. For the purposes of this book and the period we are examining, that, however, was still in the future. Suffice to say that this

period, 1907-1918, was crowned by five years of extraordinary growth and development in the assimilation of the motor vehicle into Irish society.

There is another aspect of the motor cars history which is overlooked, and that is the part it played during the Easter Rising of 1916. Both sides employed the motor vehicle with powerful effect. It gave flexibility and facilitated manoeuvrability in a way that had not been possible before. At the same time armoured vehicles were deployed in Ireland for the first time and whether or not it was the Rolls-Royce armoured cars or the cruder, but no doubt effective, improvised armoured lorries deployed by the crown forces, a new and sinister element was added to the conflict.

(144) The Heart of Dublin destroyed – 1916
Sackville Street (now O'Connell Street) and Eden Quay following the Easter Rising 1916.
Source: Author's collection

(145 Recruiting at the Mansion House, Dublin – 1915
The travelling recruiting office of the Central Recruiting Council and a B.S.A. car that was also engaged on recruiting work, photographed outside Dublin's Mansion House, the headquarters of the Council.
Source: RIAC Archive

(146) The Hospital ship 'Oxfordshire' at the North Wall – 1915
Ambulances and private cars lined up on the quayside to take newly arrived wounded soldiers from the hospital ship, 'Oxfordshire' at the North Wall, Dublin. The horses in the foreground were being loaded onto another transport ship *en route* to France.
Source: RIAC Archive

(147) T Talbot Power's Austin taking wounded soldiers to the Hospitals – 1915
Throughout 1915, a steady stream of wounded soldiers arrived in Dublin port. Here, the Austin of T Talbot Power is transporting soldiers wounded at the battle of Neuve Chapelle and newly arrived on the hospital ship 'Valdivia' to the Dublin hospitals.
Source: RIAC Archive

(148) T T L Overend's Daimler transporting wounded soldiers – 1915
The members of the Irish Automobile Club provided an almost continuous service transporting the wounded from the hospital ships arriving at Dublin port. Here, the Daimler of T T L Overend is just setting out with another group of the wounded – in this case from the hospital ship 'Valdivia'.
Source: RIAC Archive

(149) The burnt-out shell of The O'Rahilly's De Dion – 1916

The remains of The O'Rahilly's De Dion in Princes Street, Dublin. O'Rahilly (the name is a traditional title) was one of the founders of the Irish Volunteers. He opposed the Rising and tried to prevent it; when he failed, he joined the insurgents declaring: '*If the men I have trained are going into action, then I must be with them.*' His car was used for carrying arms; it was finally wrecked and ended up on a barricade. The O'Rahilly was killed on Friday, April 28th, leading a sortie from the GPO. The remains of his De Dion were buried under Hill 16 at Croke Park. *Source: RIAC Archive*

(150) Two Napier cars at the burnt-out GPO – 1916
With the cessation of hostilities, Dubliners came out to see for themselves the damage inflicted upon the heart of their city. The colonnaded building on the right, the General Post Office, had been entirely gutted and burnt out. The debris of the Hotel Metropole can be seen directly to the left of it and most of the buildings in the photograph had to be pulled down. Two Napier cars are visible in the foreground of the photograph.
Source: RIAC Archive

(151) A Wolseley delivery van converted into an Ambulance – 1915
A Wolseley delivery van which had been in use by Sir John Power and Son Limited, and which was converted into an ambulance. In the course of its conversion, Messrs. Power's engineers devised a system which allowed the stretchers to be suspended, in the process protecting the occupants from bumpy roads.
Source: RIAC Archive

(152) A nasty Experience – 1916
While attempting to travel to a session of Parliament, Lord Donoughamore and his party were travelling in a hired Ford when they were stopped in Harcourt Street, Dublin, and warned that the road ahead was dangerous. They promptly turned around but as they drove away a hail of bullets followed them, several passing through the car. One exited through the windscreen having wounded one of the occupants (note seriously) and passed through the spokes of the steering wheel. *Source: RIAC Archive*

(153) Leaving the IAC for the Royal Barracks – 1916

The work of the members of the Irish Automobile Club in operating an ambulance service is well-known. Overtaken by the events of Easter Week 1916, they continued to operate the service to all who were in need of it, often under fire. Here, one of the ambulances is seen leaving the Club house *en route* to the Royal Barracks.
Source: RIAC Archive

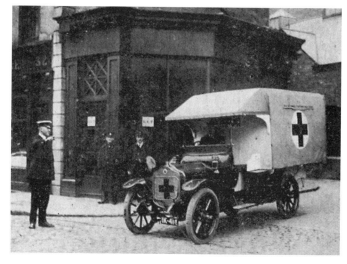

(154) A four-ton Caledon Lorry – 1916

Mr R Barry Cole of the Scottish Commercial Car Company came over from Glasgow to Dublin on Easter Monday 1916 to exhibit at the Spring Show of the Royal Dublin Society, where he had an exhibition of Caledon cars and this four-ton Caledon lorry. '*I was the witness of an exciting incident as I stood in front of the Hibernian Bank (on Sackville Street, now O'Connell Street) when a soldier in karki was taken prisoner by a party of six rebels, and it was not until this event occurred in front of me that I realised the bank was in the hands of the rebels, and when my attention was called to the armed men keeping watch from the upper windows, I decided to retire out of Dublin for the evening, but in the company of Mr C Thompson I had a further look round on the Wednesday morning and inspected from the opposite side of the river the remains of Liberty Hall. By midday on Wednesday, realising that all communication with the outside world was likely to be stopped before long, I seized the opportunity of escaping to Belfast in the company of Mr 'Barney' Briscoe in a car, kindly placed at our disposal by Mr Thompson. It took us an hour and forty minutes to get three miles from the city, owing to the numerous times we had to turn back to avoid scenes of operations. Although we gathered many alarmist accounts on the road, particularly at the prospect of meeting a large party of Sinn Feiners alleged to have been ahead of us at Balbriggan, we reached Drogheda without any trouble, being stopped several times by the constabulary and military, and from Drogheda without any difficulty in reaching Belfast, and ultimately, Glasgow.*'

The Caledon lorry, incidentally, which was left in Ballsbridge, proved invaluable for transporting fodder for the cattle and horses trapped in the Showgrounds, the vehicle working under a military escort. *Source: RIAC Archive*

(155) A Rising picture from the West – 1916

During the course of the Rising several Rolls-Royce armoured cars were deployed throughout the country. This example was photographed '*somewhere in the West*'. The Rover car is driven by Lieutenant W G Wilkinson, the Irish manager of the Rover Company, then on active service.
Source: RIAC Archive

(156) Rolls-Royce Armoured Car – 1916

Another of the fleet of Rolls-Royce armoured cars which played a part in the suppression of the 1916 Rising.
Source: RIAC Archive

(157) Some Cars that saw action during the Rising at Ashbourne – 1916
This fleet of cars belonged to McGee's Garage, Drogheda and was employed to convey wounded policemen to hospital after an attack at Ashbourne when ten of their number were killed and sixteen wounded.
Source: RIAC Archive

(158) W H Freeman at the Clontarf Barrier – 1916
W H Freeman was well known in motor sport circles being the Honorary Secretary of the Dublin and District Motor Cycle Club. He was employed as a despatch rider by the military authorities and is seen here passing the sand bag barrier erected by the military beside the Great Northern Railway line at Clontarf.
Source: RIAC Archive

(159) An Armoured car in Dublin – 1916
This improvised armoured car became a familiar sight throughout Dublin and its environs during the Easter Rising. One imagines it must have been particularly difficult to drive with its very limited vision for the driver.
Source: RIAC Archive

(160) At Bloomfield Auxiliary Hospital, Mullingar – 1917
Miss Dease, one of the staff at Bloomfield Auxiliary Hospital, Mullingar, photographed about to take a group of recovering wounded soldiers for a drive during the Summer of 1917.
Source: RIAC Archive

(161) A Ford car fitted with the 'Mak-a-Tractor' attachment – 1917

Many and varied were the devices invented to adapt the car to work on the farm. One of the key desires of inventors was to find a way to make an efficient and practical tractor. As well as purpose-built 'tractors' several ways of adapting ordinary motor cars to ploughing came into being. Our photograph shows one such device being demonstrated at the farm of Mr Lambert at Dundrum, County Dublin in 1917. This was called the 'Mak-a-Tractor' attachment and like other such inventions, came to naught with the widespread adaptation of the Ford Tractor over the next few years which clearly showed the way forward for such vehicles.

Source: RIAC Archive

(162) An old Clement car converted into a tractor – 1917

As we've already seen earlier in this book, old cars were liable to be converted into all sorts of commercial delivery vans once their prime was passed. Occasionally, they ended up providing power for some sort of farm or estate work, or, as in this case, being converted into an agricultural tractor. This old Clement was converted into a plough-pulling tractor by H Croxon of Messrs Ferguson's Dublin depot and is seen in use at Leixlip.

Source: RIAC Archive

(163) A Whiting-Bull tractor at Adare Manor – 1917

This purpose-built Whiting-Bull tractor was demonstrated at Adare Manor, the estate of the Earl of Dunraven at Adare, County Limerick in July 1917. Change comes slowly, however, to the farming community, and the *Motor News* commented '*before every farm in Ireland is aroused to the necessity of using a tractor, there must be many demonstrations of a similar character.*'
Source: RIAC Archive

(164) Running on Coal Gas – 1917

The Londonderry to Limavady Passenger Service became the first to operate one of its buses on coal gas when it introduced this Ford chassis fitted with an Olson coal gas unit in July 1917. The conversion was made by Messrs Roberts and Sons of the Foyle Street Garage, Londonderry who were regarded as the leaders in coal gas technology in Ireland at that time.
Source: RIAC Archive

TAIL-PIECE

(165) 'I wish I had an Ariel Motor' – 1908
What more can one say?
Source: RIAC Archive

BIBLIOGRAPHY

Culshaw, David & Horrobin, Peter.
 The Complete Catalogue of British Cars 1895-1975. London, Veloce, 1997.

Doyle, G. R
 The World's Automobiles 1862-1962. London, Temple Press, 1997.

Georgano, G. N.
 The Complete Encyclopaedia of Motorcars 1885-1968, New York, Dutton 1968

——, *The First Irish Roads Congress – Record of Proceedings*, Dublin, 1910

Hough, Richard.
 Tourist Trophy, London, Hutchinson, 1957

Moore, John S.
 Chambers Motors 1904-1929, Dublin, Dreoilín, 2000

Moore, John S.
 Motor Makers in Ireland. Belfast, Blackstaff Press, 1982

O'Donovan, John.
 Wheels & Deals. Dublin, Gill and Macmillan, 1983

Smith, Cornelius F.
 The History of the Royal Irish Automobile Club 1901-1991. Dublin, RIAC, 1994

Magazines & Periodicals

The Motor News
The Irish Cyclist

INDEX